NATIVE AMERICAN LEGENDS
SACAGAWEA

Don McLeese

Publishing LLC
Vero Beach, Florida 32964

www.rourkepublishing.com

PHOTO CREDITS:
©Library of Congress pgs 4, 6, 11, 12, 17
©Hulton/Archive by Getty Images Cover, pgs 18, 23, 24
©PhotoDisc, Inc. Title, pgs 9, 21
©Travel Iowa pg 15
©U.S. Treasury pg 27

Title page: *American bison were a common sight on the prairies.*

Editor: Frank Sloan

Cover and page design by Nicola Stratford

Library of Congress Cataloging-in-Publication Data

McLeese, Don.
  Sacagawea / Don McLeese.
      p. cm. -- (Native American legends)
Summary: A biography of Sacagawea, the Shoshoni Indian woman who played an important role in guiding the Lewis and Clark expedition through the Northwest Territory of the United States in 1805-1806.
Includes bibliographical references and index.
  ISBN 1-58952-729-1 (hardcover)
  1. Sacagawea—Juvenile literature. 2. Shosoni women—Biography—Juvenile literature. 3. Shoshoni Indians—Biography—Juvenile literature. 4. Lewis and Clark Expedition (1804-1806) —Juvenile literature. 5. West (U.S.)—Discovery and exploration—Juvenile literature. 6. West (U.S.)—Biography—Juvenile lierature. [1. Sacagawea. 2. Shoshoni Indians—Biography. 3. Indians of North America—Biography. 4. Women—Biography.] I. Title Native American Legends. II. Title.

  F592.7.S123M39 2003
  978'.0049745'0092—dc21

                        2003004598

Printed in the USA

W/W

Table of Contents

A Very Important Person

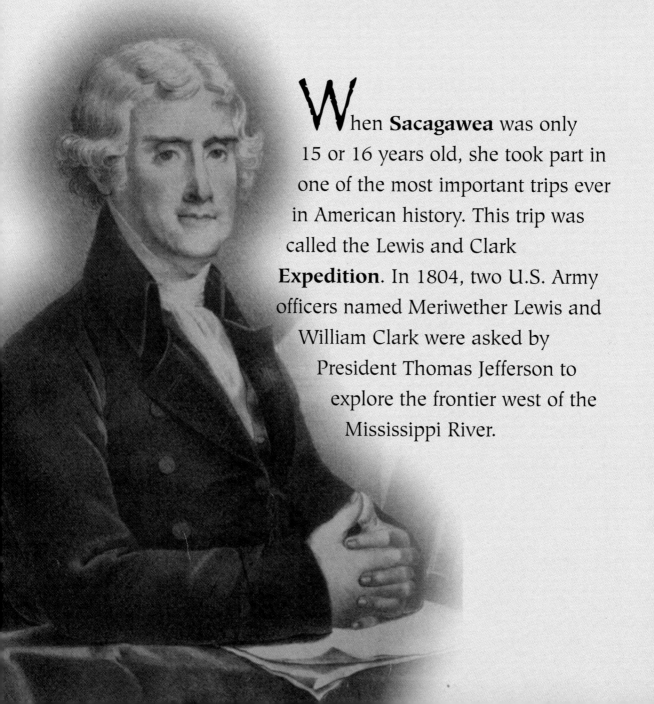

When **Sacagawea** was only 15 or 16 years old, she took part in one of the most important trips ever in American history. This trip was called the Lewis and Clark **Expedition**. In 1804, two U.S. Army officers named Meriwether Lewis and William Clark were asked by President Thomas Jefferson to explore the frontier west of the Mississippi River.

At the time, mainly Native American **tribes** lived on this land. Lewis and Clark didn't speak the languages of the tribes, so they wanted someone who did to come with them. Sacagawea was their **interpreter**. An interpreter is someone who speaks more than one language and can help people who speak different languages understand each other.

◄ *In 1803, President Jefferson was responsible for the Louisana Purchase.*

Meriwether Lewis, one half of the team of leaders of the Lewis and Clark Expedition

Because Sacagawea was a young girl, having her along would let the **Native Americans** know that Lewis and Clark didn't want to fight them. Clark wrote, "A woman in a party of men is a token of peace." Sacagawea helped Lewis and Clark make their way west, and they were able to tell President Jefferson what was out there.

After the Lewis and Clark expedition provided maps and information of the land, white settlers began moving there. Sacagawea played such a big part in the country's history that, in 2000, the United States honored her with a gold dollar coin that has her face on it.

The Louisiana Territory
In 1803, France sold the United States so much land that it made the new country twice as big. The land was 828,000 square miles (2,144,354 square kilometers) and later became 15 states. The United States paid $15 million for it.

Born a Shoshone

The baby who would grow up to be Sacagawea was probably born in 1790. Because the Native Americans didn't write these things down, some history books say she might have been born in 1788 or 1789. She was the daughter of a **chief** of the **Shoshone** tribe. Her tribe lived in the Rocky Mountains in what is now Idaho.

When she was a baby, she had a name that meant "Grass Maiden." It wasn't until later that she became known as Sacagawea, which means "Bird Woman." She was small and she moved quickly, just like a bird.

Native American Names
Most Native Americans were given a different name as a baby than their later name. As they grew up, they would get a name that told what they were like.

A modern photograph showing the beauty of Sacagawea's home ➤
state of Idaho

In 1800, when she was only 10 years old, her tribe was attacked by another tribe, the **Hidatsa**. The Shoshone tribe had come down from the Rocky Mountains to hunt buffalo for food in what is now Montana. The Hidatsa tribe wanted the same land and buffalo, so they started fighting. The Hidatsa tribe had guns, and the Shoshone tribe only had bows and arrows.

Fifteen members of the Shoshone tribe died, and the rest ran away. The girl known as Grass Maiden tried to run away but was taken by a Hidatsa warrior.

The Hidatsa took her hundreds of miles from the home she knew in the Rocky Mountains and gave her to a new family. This must have been very scary, but she was a brave little girl.

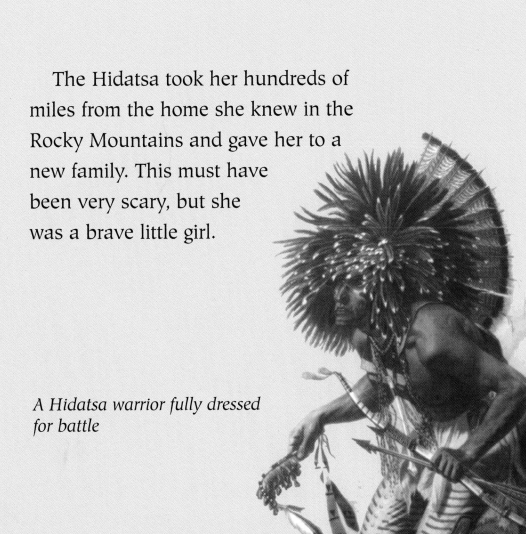

A Hidatsa warrior fully dressed for battle

An Indian man, woman, and child shown with a fur trader

A Child Wife

It was only a year or two later when a fur trader from Canada named **Toussaint Charbonneau** saw the girl for the first time. By now, she was called Sacagawea. Even though she was only 11 or 12, and he was at least three times as old, he wanted her to be his wife.

Charbonneau traded the skins of animals that he trapped for food or anything else he wanted. He asked Sacagawea's new family if he could trade for her. They said yes. Sacagawea didn't have any choice and now had to live with another stranger.

Lewis and Clark

In May of 1804, Lewis and Clark began their expedition. They and their company of 43 men took three boats from St. Louis on the Missouri River and went north and west. In late October, they reached what is now North Dakota. This is where Charbonneau and Sacagawea were living.

Meriwether Lewis and William Clark
Meriwether Lewis was 29 years old when he was asked to lead the expedition by his friend, President Jefferson. Lewis asked 33-year-old William Clark to go with him and to pick the other men for the journey.

A modern photograph of a boat used by Lewis and Clark ➤

Lewis and Clark needed someone who could talk to the Native American tribes, and Charbonneau said he could. Not only could he talk the language, but his wife was a Native American. Since Lewis and Clark wanted to get some horses from the Shoshone tribe, Sacagawea could be a big help. Lewis and Clark paid the two of them $500 to come.

"Pomp"

Though Sacagawea was only 15 years old when she met Lewis and Clark, she was pregnant with her first child. Before they left, she gave birth to a baby boy on February 11, 1805. Her husband named his son **Jean Baptiste Charbonneau.** William Clark called the baby "Pomp," which became his nickname. In the Shoshone language, Pomp meant "First Born" or "Little Chief."

A Native American mother and her papoose ➤

Papoose
Native Americans often called a baby a **papoose**. A mother would carry her papoose in a pack on her back until the infant was old enough to walk.

Heading Home

On April 7, the expedition started again on the Missouri River. Sacagawea carried two-month-old Pomp on her back. For Sacagawea, going west with Lewis and Clark meant going home. She was heading back toward the land where she had been taken from the Shoshone. She hadn't seen her family and friends in five years! On the trip, they had some bad weather and Sacagawea got sick, but they kept going. She helped the expedition find food and find its way.

Namesakes
Many of the places Sacagawea visited on her trip are now named after her. These include lakes in Washington and North Dakota, mountains in Idaho, Wyoming, Montana, and Oregon, and a river in Montana.

◄ *Lewis, Clark, and Sacagawea on the famous expedition*

In August of 1805, the expedition came to the place that Sacagawea knew was home. They met some Shoshone women, who were afraid that Lewis and Clark's soldiers wanted to fight the tribe. But when the tribe saw that Sacagawea was with them, they knew that there wouldn't be a fight. They took Sacagawea to meet their chief.

When she saw him, she started crying with joy. The chief was her brother, **Cameahwait**. He was very happy to see her as well. She told her brother that Lewis and Clark wanted to trade for horses to continue their journey. The expedition company would give the tribe clothing, knives, and other things for the horses.

Because her brother trusted Sacagawea, he gave Lewis and ➤
Clark wild horses like these shown here.

Shoshone Horses
The Shoshone tribe was known to raise great horses, which the Native Americans rode when they were traveling and hunting. From the start of their expedition, Lewis and Clark wanted to find the tribe so they could trade for horses.

Going West

Sacagawea could have stayed with the Shoshone, the tribe that was her family. But Lewis and Clark needed to keep going west, and she decided to keep going with them. They had been very kind to her and to Pomp. She felt like a very important part of the expedition.

Except for her brother, the chief, most of her family had died during the time she was away from the Shoshone. She would be able to meet other Native American tribes and even see the ocean. In late August, Sacagawea and the expedition said good-bye to the Shoshone.

A painting of Sacagawea that shows her interpreting for ➤
members of the expedition

The Big Water

The expedition could never have kept going without the horses that Sacagawea helped them get from the Shoshone tribe. The soldiers rode the horses until they reached rivers that would take them by canoe to the **Pacific Ocean**. Many Native Americans called this ocean the "Big Water."

Sacagawea's greatest fame came with her work for Lewis and Clark.

Tribes that they met on the trip knew that Lewis and Clark came in peace, because they had Sacagawea and baby Pomp with them. As Clark wrote in his journal, "No woman ever accompanies a war party."

In November, they finally reached the ocean. Sacagawea had traveled with the expedition more than 2,000 miles (3,219 kilometers) to see it!

Pacific Ocean
The biggest body of water in the world is at the western edge of the United States.

The Rest of Her Life

Sacagawea had helped make the Lewis and Clark expedition a great success. In March, 1806, the expedition started heading back to St. Louis.

Some history books say that Sacagawea and Pomp went to St. Louis as well. Others say that they returned to the Rocky Mountains to live with the Shoshone. No one is even sure when she died. Some say 1812, when she was only 22. Others say she lived to be 94, and died in 1884.

All agree that the help Sacagawea gave Lewis and Clark was an important part of American history.

The gold dollar coin with Sacagawea and baby Pomp ➤

The Sacagawea Dollar
This gold coin with Sacagawea and Pomp on the front honors her for her help with Lewis and Clark.

Born to the Lemhi Shoshones, Sacagawea was probably about 11 when she was kidnapped by another tribe, the Hidatsa. But she always thought of herself as Shoshone. The Shoshone were among the Great Basin People, who lived in what are now the states of Nevada, Colorado, Utah, Wyoming, Idaho, and eastern California.

Today the Western Shoshone number about 500 Gosiute, and there are about 3,500 Western Shoshone who live on or near the Fort Hall Reservation in Idaho. About 2,500 Eastern Shoshone live on Wind River Reservation in Wyoming.

Time Line

1790?	Sacagawea is born.
1800	The Hidatsa tribe kidnaps Sacagawea in an attack on the Shoshone tribe.
1803	United States pays $15 million to France for the Louisiana Purchase.
1804	Lewis and Clark are asked to explore west of the Mississippi.
1805	Sacagawea gives birth to her son, Jean Baptiste ("Pomp") Charbonneau and joins the Lewis and Clark expedition.
1806	Lewis and Clark head back to St. Louis.
1812 or 1884	Sacagawea dies
2000	The United States issues the Sacagawea gold dollar coin

Glossary

Cameahwait (cah MEE ah wate) — Sacagawea's brother, chief of the Shoshone tribe

chief (CHEEF) — leader, head of a Native American tribe

expedition (ecks peh DIH shun) — a trip to explore, or a journey with some other purpose

Hidatsa (hih DAT suh) — a tribe of Native Americans

interpreter (inn TURR pruh ter) — someone who speaks more than one language and can help people who speak different languages understand each other

Jean Baptiste Charbonneau (jhan bap TEEST CHAR buh no) — Sacagawea's son, nicknamed "Pomp"

Native Americans (NAY tiv uh MARE ih cans) — those who lived in the land that is now the United States before explorers from Europe came

Pacific Ocean (puh SIFF ick OH shun) — the world's largest body of water, at the western edge of the United States

papoose (paah POOS) — a Native American baby or young child

Sacagawea (sah kah ga WEE ah *or* sah kah ja WEE ah) — Native American woman

Shoshone (shuh SHOW nee) — a tribe of Native Americans

Toussaint Charbonneau (too SAHN CHAR buh no) — Sacagawea's husband

tribes (TRYBZ) — bands or nations of Native Americans

Further Reading

Alter, Judy. *Sacagawea: Native American Interpreter.* The Child's World, Inc., 2002

Fradin, Dennis Brindell. *Who Was Sacagawea?* Penguin Putnam Books for Young Readers, 2002

Krensky, Stephen. *Sacagawea and the Bravest Deed.* Aladdin Paperbacks, 2002

Websites to Visit

www.pbs.org/lewisandclark/inside/saca.html

www.usmint.gov/mint_programs/golden_dollar_coin/index.cfm?flash=yes&action=about_sacagawea

www.pbs.org/weta/thewest/people/s_z/sacagawea.htm

Index

About The Author

Don McLeese is an award-winning journalist whose work has appeared in many newspapers and magazines. He earned his M.A. degree in English from the University of Chicago, taught feature writing at the University of Texas and has frequently contributed to the World Book Encyclopedia. He lives with his wife and two daughters in West Des Moines, Iowa.